THE GOOD GOLF GUIDE

IMPROVE
YOUR SHORT GAME

This material previously appeared in *Improve Your Golf*.
This volume compiled by Paul Foston and Sally Hiller.

3295
Published in 1994 by Tiger Books International PLC, London
in association with CLB Publishing, Godalming, Surrey
© Eaglemoss Publications Ltd 1989, 1990, 1991, 1992
All rights reserved
Printed and bound in Hong Kong
ISBN 1-85501-414-9

THE GOOD GOLF GUIDE

IMPROVE
YOUR SHORT GAME

TIGER BOOKS INTERNATIONAL
LONDON

CONTENTS

INTRODUCTION

It is surprising how few people take the time and effort to improve their short game, concentrating instead on power play, without appreciating that it is frequently the short shots that ruin their score.

What is the difference between chipping and pitching? To chip and run or to chip and stop? Which club do I use? These are important questions to consider if you are to become competent around the greens.

In order to have a reliable short game, you will need to develop your touch around the greens; this requires both feel and imagination, as well as the ability sometimes to play a shot from the most awkward of positions.

The following carefully selected situations will help you to visualise the shots beforehand, so that you can execute them with consistency.

The next time you go to the practice ground, take a few of the clubs we recommend and try out the drills. Keep repeating the strokes and you will soon build a solid short game.

Nick Price chips with a 7 iron during the 1985 USPGA Championship.

DEVELOP YOUR TOUCH

You can't expect to hit every green in regulation, but you can learn to get up and down in two from around the green. If you are to score consistently you will need to develop a deft touch. To help you we have selected different types of shots for various situations. Knowing what club to use in a given situation can be a real advantage.

Colin Montgomerie shows confidence in his ability by choosing to lob the ball from the fringe of the green instead of opting to chip and run.

Chipping around the green

A chip is a stroke played from between 5yd (4 m) and 30yd (27m) of the green. The aim of a chip is to get your ball close enough to the hole so that your next shot is simply a tap-in with the putter. Good chipping can save you at least half-a-dozen strokes per round. With regular practice you'll find your chipping improves dramatically.

The chip is a short shot you play with two-thirds swing or less and it needs a deft touch to do it well. Although you can chip with any iron from a 5 down to a sand wedge – depending on the length of the shot and the obstacles to clear – this chapter concentrates on

PICKING THE SHOT

The type of chip you play depends on the situation you find yourself in. Assess the lie of the land for how far the ball can fly and how far you want it to roll. As a general rule

three of the most common types of chip using the 7 iron; 9 iron; and sand wedge.

WHICH CHIP?

Before choosing your chip, you must consider three factors: how high the ball needs to fly; how far it has to fly; and how far it can roll.

As a general rule you should always try to run the ball along the ground for as great a distance as the terrain permits, since there is less chance of the shot going wrong on the ground than in the air.

If the ground is relatively flat and even and there are no obsta-

always try to run the ball along the ground for as far as possible. This is easier and safer than trying to stop the ball quickly with a more lofted club.

cles to clear, then a low-flying chip and run is best. Play this shot using a clubface with little loft, such as a medium iron, so that the ball travels in a low trajectory (curving flight path through the air). The ball spends one-third of its journey in the air and the remaining two-thirds rolling along the ground.

If there is an obstacle to clear between you and the green but there is still quite a way for the ball to roll, play a medium height chip using a short iron. With this shot the ball spends roughly equal parts of its journey in the air and on the ground.

The ground between your ball and the green may be uneven with humps, bunkers or an irregular surface, and with not much level ground to the pin for the ball to roll over. In this case you want the ball to spend nearly all its time in

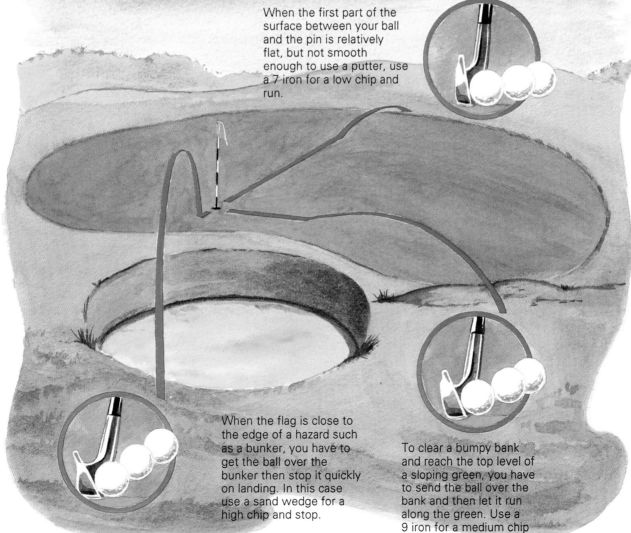

When the first part of the surface between your ball and the pin is relatively flat, but not smooth enough to use a putter, use a 7 iron for a low chip and run.

When the flag is close to the edge of a hazard such as a bunker, you have to get the ball over the bunker then stop it quickly on landing. In this case use a sand wedge for a high chip and stop.

To clear a bumpy bank and reach the top level of a sloping green, you have to send the ball over the bank and then let it run along the green. Use a 9 iron for a medium chip and run.

7 IRON CHIP AND RUN

1 AT ADDRESS
Use a putting grip down the handle. Move your left foot about 2in (5cm) back to open your stance but align your upper body parallel. Clubface aim is square to target. Your weight favours the left.

2 BACKSWING AND IMPACT
Do not break your wrists on the backswing. The clubhead reaches no higher than knee level at the top of the backswing. The swing is a pendulum movement similar to a crisp putting stroke.

3 THROUGHSWING
Your shoulders, arms and hands move as one during the whole stroke. Do not break your wrists on the throughswing which is as long as the backswing. Your left shoulder rises after impact.

the air before stopping quickly. Play a shot – commonly known as the chip and stop – where you send the ball high with a club that has a big loft angle, such as a sand wedge. With this shot the ball is in the air for at least two-thirds of its route.

CHIPPING BASICS

Regardless of the stroke you play and the club you use there are a few basics that apply to all chipping strokes. For a start, your back and throughswing are the same length. At the same time you need a longer back and throughs wing the further you have to chip. The slightest change in clubhead speed makes a great difference to the result of the shot. Practice will help you learn a feel for the ball and teach you how far you have to swing.

Another common feature of all chip shots is aligning your lower body left of the ball-to-target line. An open (aligned left) lower body prevents your hips from obstructing your hands at impact. For proper chip alignment take a normal parallel stance, and then slide your left foot back about 2in (5cm) to open your stance and align left.

However, you must still align your upper body parallel to the ball-to-target line. Also, the aim of the clubhead is always square on to the ball-to-target line.

THREE USEFUL CHIPS

Around the green there are three common situations you might find

yourself in. Each calls for a different chip. The first is where your ball is lying just off the green beyond the apron. Here you use a 7 iron and a low chip and run. Where your ball is slightly further away, with perhaps a bank in the way you can chip with a 9 iron. Finally, where

9 IRON MEDIUM CHIP

1 AT ADDRESS
Hold the club with a normal grip but still down the handle. Otherwise address the ball the same as for a 7 iron chip and run.

Chip tip
When you are playing a short chip and run, the stroke is crisp and firm and your wrists must not move forward of the clubhead. Lift your left shoulder on the throughswing.

your ball is lying with a bunker or some other hazard in the way and the hole is close to the hazard, use a sand wedge to play a high chip and stop to bring your ball close to the hole.

7 IRON LOW CHIP

Use this shot when there are no obstacles to clear and there is a large area of even ground for the ball to roll along. The ball travels two-thirds of its distance on the ground and only one-third of it in the air.

To play this shot, hold the club with a putting grip and grip down the handle. Aim the clubface square on to the ball-to-target line and adopt an open stance. Position the ball in the centre of your stance.

Do not break your wrists on the backswing, and let your shoulders, arms and hands move in unison during the whole movement. This produces a smooth action which should be short and crisp.

The swing is, in effect, like a crisper version of the putting stroke. By using the putting grip you eliminate wrist action. Try to imagine your swing as a pendulum motion with an equal length back and throughswing.

Your shoulders, arms and hands move as one unit from start to finish and the clubhead stays

IN THE AIR AND ON THE GROUND

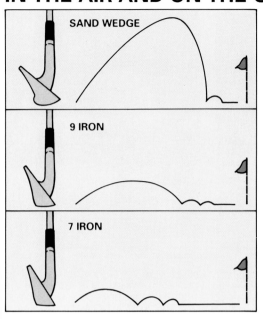

To help you select the right club for the chip remember that in a 7 iron chip the ball travels about two thirds of its journey rolling along the ground; with a 9 iron chip the ball is on the ground for half its journey; with a sand wedge chip and stop it is on the ground only for the last third of its journey.

square to the ball-to-target line during most of the stroke, only moving inside this line at the furthest point in both backswing and throughswing.

After impact allow your left shoulder to lift up. This stops your wrist from breaking and keeps the clubface square to the ball-to-target line for most of the followthrough.

The clubhead approaches the ball at a shallow angle, crisply sweeping it off the turf. This puts top spin on to maximize roll.

9 IRON MEDIUM CHIP

Use a 9 iron to produce a medium chip when the ball needs to be hit high enough to clear an obstacle, but doesn't need to stop quickly on landing. The curve of the ball is higher than that of a 7 iron – although it doesn't run as far along the ground.

With this chip use your normal grip but still grip down the handle. Set the clubface and address the ball in the same way as for the 7 iron chip.

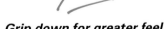

Grip down for greater feel
You can improve your feel, and achieve greater clubhead control and awareness, by gripping down the handle. The closer your hands are to the clubhead, the better touch you have, and the more accurate your shot.

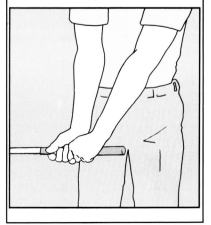

2 BACKSWING
Break your wrists a little on the backswing and swing the clubhead to about waist height. Backswing is equal length to throughswing.

3 IMPACT AND ON
Allow your left shoulder to rise after impact so as not to let your clubhead overtake your hands. Hold your followthrough position.

SAND WEDGE HIGH CHIP AND STOP

1 AT ADDRESS
Adopt the same grip and stance as you would for a 9 iron chip. Distribute your body weight evenly over both feet.

2 BACK AND DOWN
Allow your wrists to break at the start of the backswing which should be about two-thirds the length of your normal full swing.

3 IMPACT AND THROUGH
Your right hand must stay underneath the shaft to prevent any wrist roll. As you follow through, rotate to face the target.

This time let your wrists break a little during the backswing. At the top of the backswing your clubhead should reach no higher than hip level. The clubface attacks the ball at a steeper angle than the 7 iron and the clubhead follows a normal in-to-in swingpath.

Hold your followthrough and don't allow your wrists to break after impact. Let your left shoulder rise on the followthrough. As you complete the throughswing allow your upper body to rotate towards the target.

SAND WEDGE HIGH CHIP

Use the sand wedge to play the chip and stop. Select this club when the nearest landing point beyond a hazard is very close to the target – and when there is very little room for the ball to run. The sand wedge produces a high curve and creates backspin to stop the ball quickly. However, it is the least easy chip to perform because you have only a small area in which to land and stop the ball.

Grip the club and address the ball in the same way as you would for a 9 iron chip.

Let your left wrist break almost immediately as you start the swing. Your backswing is about two-thirds of the length of your normal swing. On the downswing the

clubhead approaches impact at an acute angle, but don't let your hands overtake the clubface at any time.

Do not break your wrists through impact. Feel that your right hand is a passenger staying underneath the shaft as you strike. Your upper body turns to face the target at the completion of the followthrough.

CHIPPING PRACTICE

If you want to develop a good short game you must practise these strokes regularly. Not only do you need to learn the different techniques involved, but you have to acquire a feel for the shots. It is a general rule in golf that the shorter the shot, the more precise you must be and the greater feel you must have.

One good practice routine is to chip into an umbrella. Place the umbrella at the point where you want the ball to land. Position it at different distances and practise with different clubs – especially the sand wedge.

Another useful chipping practice aid is a chipping net. Use it in the same way as you would an umbrella, changing the distance away from you so you build up feel for the amount of swing needed.

When you become consistent at landing the ball in the umbrella or net, you are halfway to being a good chipper. The other half is achieved by correctly visualizing the shot – knowing where to land the ball and how it runs.

Clubface control
To ensure that you do not flick at the ball through impact, your right hand stays under the shaft during impact and followthrough.

Sand wedge around the green

Balanced downhill stance

Most amateurs use their sand wedge around the green from only a bunker or rough grass. But there is great scope for a variety of shots to be played with the same club. Instead of using clubs from the 7 iron upwards for different situations it's possible to manufacture every greenside chip shot with a sand wedge.

It's not for everyone, but the advantage of using the same club for nearly every situation is that you can cultivate good feel and touch. By regularly playing the sand wedge you know instinctively how the ball behaves whatever way you use the club. This helps your confidence. Chipping with a different club each

HAZARDOUS LOB
Because the sand wedge is the most lofted club in the bag it's perfect for delicate lobs. Facing a chip over trouble from a downhill lie, position the ball slightly further back in your stance – to help avoid the thin – and choke down the grip. Try to tilt with the slope and push your weight forward to be sturdy. If the slope is steep, press on the inside of your back foot for balance. Pick the club up quickly with plenty of wrist break (above) to follow the contours of the slope. A steep attack also helps the ball to gain height.

time makes judging the shot tricky – shaft length and loft vary with each club.

Playing the sand wedge in most situations also forces you to be creative each time. It helps you to visualize shots effectively, not only around the green but in every department of your game.

CHANGING CHIPS

The various sand wedge shots – perhaps a chip and run or high lob over trouble – are easy to play. Slightly alter your ball position, stance, clubface loft and type of swing.

The **long chip and run** shot is usually associated with a straighter faced club like a 7 or 8 iron but a sand wedge can be used just as effectively. Place the ball well back in the stance and push your hands forward, taking loft off the clubface.

Play the stroke with a firm wristed action – strike down crisply on the ball, and don't quit. The ball flies much lower than a conventional sand wedge, then checks on the second bounce and runs up to the hole.

Use the same technique for the **short chip over a fringe**. Most golfers opt for a putter, but sometimes there's a risk of an irregular roll through the grass and so pace is difficult to judge – especially on fast greens. A little bump off the back foot with a sand wedge lifts the ball just enough to clear the fringe and the ball rolls towards the pin. You may be surprised how often you hole out once you have thoroughly practised this technique.

The **low running** sand wedge can also replace the 8 iron for a bump and run up a slope to a flag cut just on the green. Instead of pinning trust on the ball bouncing several times up the slope, you can play a sand wedge so that it bounces only once or twice, lessening the risk of the shot taking bad hops. But the sand wedge shot has to be played precisely so practise the stroke before you attempt it on the course.

The one time you should hit another club is when you're faced with a chip off hard bare ground. The danger of thinning or fluffing the shot outweighs any advantage gained. Reach instead for a straighter faced club.

ONE FOR ALL

BUMP AND RUN
Don't be afraid of using the sand wedge from just off the green instead of a straight faced iron or putter – it's a simple shot to play. Position the ball well back in your stance – opposite the right foot – and push your hands forward to deloft the clubface. Push your weight forward also. With a firm wristed putting action strike down firmly on the ball – it pops up to clear the fringe but flies low enough so that it runs on landing.

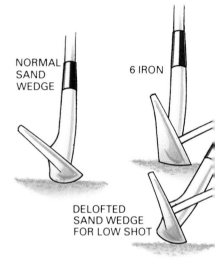

NORMAL SAND WEDGE

6 IRON

DELOFTED SAND WEDGE FOR LOW SHOT

CHECKING CHIP
An 8 iron is a good choice for a chip over a medium sized fringe provided the target is far enough away – the ball runs on landing. A sand wedge can be played like an 8 iron, but the shot checks more on landing. This gives you extra control but the ball still rolls, which is especially useful on fast greens or going downhill.

8 IRON

SAND WEDGE WITH 8 IRON LOFT

DELICATE TOUCH
A chip over a large fringe with little green to work with is a perfect situation for the sand wedge. A pitching wedge is fine but needs to be played very precisely for the ball to go close. The sand wedge gains more height and lands softly so you can afford to be slightly bolder. But think again about using the lob with the sand wedge if it has to be played from hard pan. The pitching wedge is then the better option.

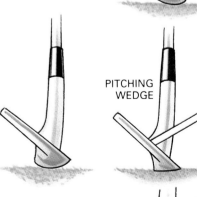

PITCHING WEDGE

SAND WEDGE LANDS SOFTLY

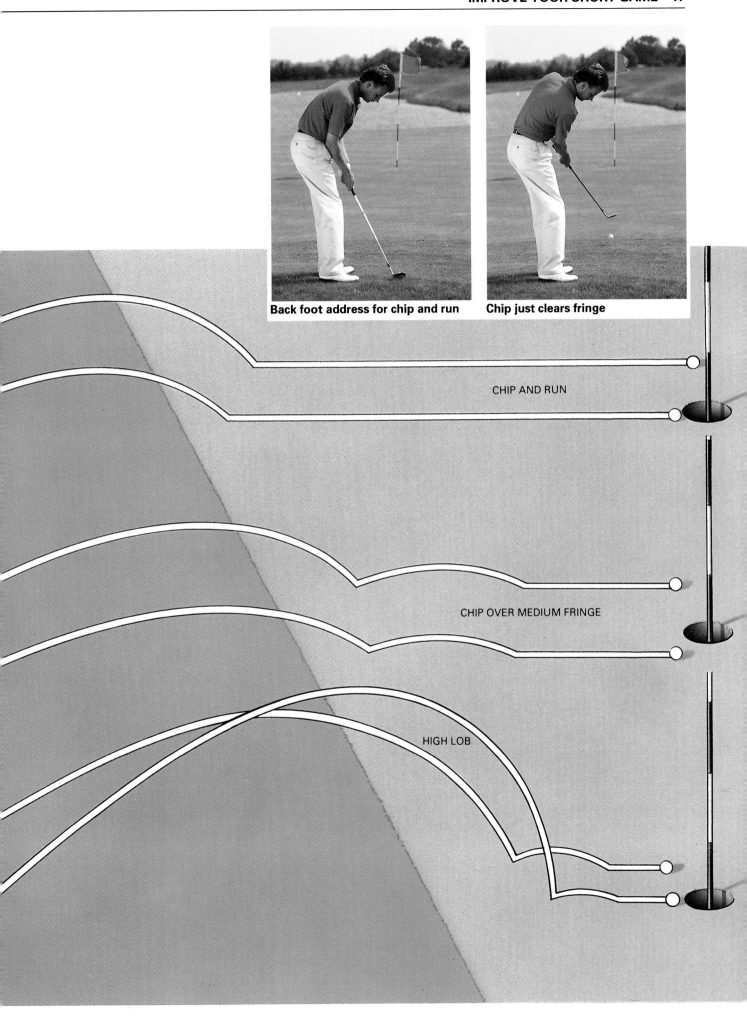

Back foot address for chip and run

Chip just clears fringe

CHIP AND RUN

CHIP OVER MEDIUM FRINGE

HIGH LOB

Fringe play

Even top professionals don't hit every green in regulation, so they spend hours practising the art of fringe play. They fully appreciate that the ability to get up and down in two is just as important as striking the full shots well.

Fringe grass is evenly cut and similar in length to light rough. A chip from the fringe is a short shot – there's seldom more than 30yd (27m) between you and the flag.

Unlike most other shots in golf, there are no obstacles in front of you to worry about.

STROKE SAVERS

There's more than one way to play a chip from the fringe and every one is a potential stroke saver. It's vital you understand which club is best suited to any given situation, so try not to restrict your-

CHIP AWAY AT YOUR SCORE
Intelligent club selection and knowing how the ball reacts from different lies are just as important for the short game as a correct technique. A low running chip is a safe shot likely to give you consistent results. Don't lob the ball high into the air from short range unless you have very little green to work with.

CHIP AND RUN OFF FRINGE

1 SQUARE ON
When there's plenty of green between you and the flag the ideal shot is the chip and run. Select a spot on the green where you intend to pitch the ball. The ball is in contact with the ground for most of its journey, so consider the speed and slope of the green – the roll of the ball is influenced by both.
Stand square to the target with the ball central in your stance. Keep your hands ahead of the clubhead at address – they should remain that way throughout the swing.

2 SLOWLY BACK
Take the club away from the ball smoothly and break the wrists only a little. The length of backswing determines the length of the shot. Feel your left hand in complete control of the club – the right hand acts mainly in a supporting role for a shot as short as this.

3 NUDGE FORWARD
The left hand leads the clubhead down on a shallow angle of attack into the bottom of the ball. Keep the hands ahead of the clubhead at all times to prevent the dreaded scooping action at impact. Don't worry about getting the ball airborne – the loft of the club does this for you. This is a simple back and through movement with the hands and arms.
Don't hit down sharply at the ball – neither height nor backspin are required for this shot.

4 BALL RUNS UP TO HOLE
Long after the ball is on its way to the hole your left hand should be held ahead of the clubhead. Concentrate on keeping the clubface pointing at the target. The ball pitches less than halfway to the flag and runs up to the hole. A successful chip leaves you a very makeable putt for your next shot.

HIGH AND SHORT

1 HANDS AHEAD
When the ball sits down in fringe grass and there's very little green to work with, a sand wedge is the club for the job. Adopt an open stance with the ball back in your stance and your hands forward.

2 STEEP BACK
Break the wrists very early in the backswing – the sideways movement of the hands is tiny but the hinge effect of the wrists gives you enough length on the backswing.

self to a personal favourite.

Check the lie of the ball, the distance between you and the flag and the ground conditions on the green – these three factors determine the club you should use. Let your imagination work in your favour – select a spot where you want the ball to pitch and visualize it running up towards the hole.

Take a couple of practice swings to develop a feel for the shot you've chosen. These swings help you focus your mind on the task in hand and prevent you rushing in too hastily.

FLOAT SHOT

When the ball sits down in a fluffy lie and there's not much green to work with, you're faced with a difficult chip. But a sound technique and sensible club selection help you out of trouble every time. You need to generate clubhead speed to avoid the duffed shot while at the same time taking care not to overhit the ball.

Reach for your sand wedge and stand open to the ball-to-target line.

Lay the clubface open in your stance so that it aims squarely at the flag. Adopt a weak left hand grip to prevent the clubface closing during the swing. Break the wrists quickly on the backswing and cut down across the ball from out to in. Like taking sand with a bunker shot, you rely on the grass acting as a cushion at impact. The ball pops up in the air, lands softly on the green and runs very little.

If you're fortunate enough to find your ball in a good lie, this is altogether a much easier shot. The ball may fly up a little higher – and so run less – but exactly the same techniques apply.

LOW RUNNER

When there's plenty of green between you and the flag, a shot with a lower trajectory is required. If the lie is good use an 8 iron – you want the ball to travel in the air for less than half of its journey to the hole.

Select a spot on the green where you aim to pitch the ball. Gauge the slope of the green – the ball runs

along the ground for most of the way and takes any breaks in the same way as a putt. Set up fairly square to the target and position the ball towards the centre of your stance.

Swing your arms back and through, keeping the left wrist firm and dominant. The ball is lofted over the fringe on to the putting surface and runs smoothly up towards the hole.

From a poor lie use a more lofted club, perhaps a 9 iron. The techniques which served you well from a good lie help you again in this slightly trickier situation. Address the ball in exactly the same way. Make sure your hands are ahead of the ball – all types of chipping faults can stem from positioning your hands behind the ball.

Swing back with a small amount of wrist break and accelerate the clubhead down into the bottom of the ball. Grass comes between the clubface and the ball, so don't concern yourself with backspin. The ball comes out quite low and runs a long way.

3 RETURN TO ADDRESS
Grass acts as a cushion at impact – as sand does on a bunker shot – so accelerate on the downswing. The importance of a correct set-up becomes clear as you return to exactly the same position as address.

4 SOFT TOUCH
This is a perfect example of the paradox of hitting down on the ball to gain height on the shot – the natural loft of the club pops the ball up in the air. Your head remains perfectly still throughout.

Rules check
With a putter in your hands it's easy to mark and lift your ball simply out of habit – but you risk breaking the rules if you do so when your ball has come to rest on the fringe.

Most courses allow you this luxury only when winter rules are in force, so check the noticeboard in the clubhouse before you step on to the course. An infringement of this rule costs you a hole in matchplay and 2 penalty shots in strokeplay.

5 LEFT IN CHARGE
Notice how dominant the left hand is even though the ball is well on its travels – at no time in the shot is the clubhead allowed to overtake the hands. The ball lands softly on the green and runs very little.

CLOSELY CUT

The apron tends to be only a few paces wide and skirts around every green between the fringe and the putting surface. The grass is just slightly longer than you find on the green – for this reason your putter is usually the most effective club. The ball is always in contact with the ground, so you eliminate the risk of an uneven bounce.

If the apron is damp from early morning dew or rain, a shot with a 7 iron using your putting stroke can produce excellent results. Your stance, grip and ball position remain the same as if you were holding a putter. A smooth stroke gently lofts the ball over the apron, preventing any dampness slowing it down.

FRINGE BENEFITS

More than half of your shots in a round of golf are chips and putts, so at least half of your practice should be devoted to this aspect of the game.

You can spend hours practising your short game and not become in the least bit tired – chipping requires little physical effort.

To make your practice enjoyable vary the type of shot you play. Experiment with different clubs and learn to understand how the ball reacts.

In the winter months you can also practise your putting indoors – and even some gentle chipping with an air ball. With enough practice you are certain to develop into an accomplished chipper of the ball – your scores are bound to tumble as a result.

Reach for an iron
If your ball is nestling down slightly in the fringe grass you can use any club from a 7 iron to a pitching wedge. The club you choose depends on the amount of green you have to work with. A good maxim to remember is less green/more loft, and more green/less loft.

Don't putt
Even if you're close to the flag, rule out any hope of using a putter from this lie – it usually leads to disaster. The straight face of the putter is totally unsuited to playing from the fluffy grass on the fringe. Pace is almost impossible to judge so take a lofted club instead.

APRON PUTTER

Not all putters are suited to apron play. Use one that gives a smooth roll – if the ball jumps into the air on impact it's likely to pull up short.

An **offset** putter lofts the ball slightly at impact – though the ball is briefly in the air it rolls smoothly once on the green.

A **mallet** putter isn't suited to apron play. The ball hops at impact – speed is lost and the putt pulls up short of the hole.

A conventional **blade** putter is ideal. Struck from the sweet spot the ball runs smoothly along the ground towards the hole.

Avoid a **centre shafted** putter. The ball jumps into the air and you can't judge pace accurately.

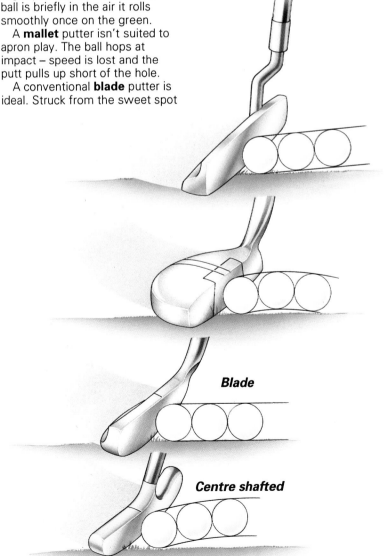

Blade

Centre shafted

THE ART OF PITCHING

Pitching is definitely an art. If you are to set up birdie chances on par fives, or save par after a poor tee shot, you will need to develop the art of pitching. We look at a variety of pitch shots that are especially useful from 120 yards in.

**Manuel Pinero plays a punched pitch –
a low shot with lots of backspin that
stops on the second bounce.**

Pitching

For a pitch shot, the ball is hit high and travels further in the air than along the ground. A pitch is an extension of both the medium and high chip shots and is played between 35yd (32m) and 100yd (91m) from the green.

The aim of a pitch is to play the ball close enough to the hole so that your next shot is a short putt. To play it well requires a lot of practice as well as a fine touch, but once you've mastered it you could save yourself several shots per round.

The pitch is a feel shot played with no more than a three-quarter swing and with any one of a number of clubs. The most common are the sand wedge, pitching wedge and 9 iron.

CHOOSING YOUR CLUB

The club you use depends on the distance of the shot. The sand wedge, with a clubface loft of about 56°, is for shots of 35-60yd (32-55m) while a pitching wedge (with a loft of about 50°) is for 61-80yd (56-73m) strikes. A 9 iron (about 46° loft) hits the ball 81-100yd (74-91m) with a three-quarter swing.

These distances increase as you improve. But whatever the distance of the shot and whichever club you use, your tempo must stay the same.

The technique is the same for

PITCHING TO YOUR TARGET
The pitch is a high shot played with a lofted club – the ball spends more time in the air than rolling along the ground. The key to a successful pitch is to keep your left hand, wrist and arm firm at impact.

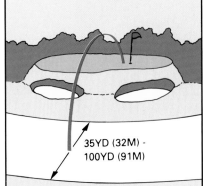

35YD (32M) -
100YD (91M)

The pitching zone
The pitch shot is played to a target between 35yd (32m) and 100yd (91m) away – and even further as your game improves. You have to hit the ball high from this distance because you are too far away to play the chip and run – even if there are no hazards between your ball and the target.

Vary your swing length

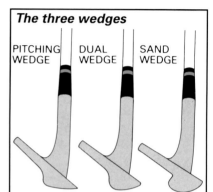

Providing you keep the same tempo for all shots, the length of your swing determines how far you hit the ball. To develop a feel for distance, vary your swing from half to two-thirds to three-quarters when practising – but keep the same tempo for each stroke.

each club – although the swing plane changes slightly according to the length of the shaft. The shorter the shaft the more your back is bent and the more upright the swing plane is. The sand wedge has a steeper swing plane than either the pitching wedge or the 9 iron.

ADDRESS AND SWING

Hold the club about 2in (5cm) down the shaft with the standard overlap grip. Take a slightly open stance with your left foot about 2in (5cm) behind your right, so that your hands and arms can swing freely through impact. However, your hips, chest and shoulders remain parallel to the ball-to-target line.

Your stance is slightly wider than if playing a chip and run. The ball is midway between your feet.

Let your left wrist break immediately you start the takeaway. This helps create a steep back-swing and moves your hands and arms into the correct position to start the downswing.

Your left hand must stay ahead of the clubface on the downswing, and pull it into the ball. Keep both

hands, your wrists and arms firm as you hit the ball. At impact, both hands are still slightly ahead of the clubface – it is only after impact that it moves level with your hands. Your right hand stays behind the left for as long as possible.

It's vital to remember that your left hand dominates the swing,

The three wedges

PITCHING WEDGE   DUAL WEDGE   SAND WEDGE

In addition to the sand wedge and pitching wedge, there is a dual wedge which combines the qualities of both. Its loft angle is midway between the two – and it has a rounded sole for bunker play. If you have all three clubs in your bag, practise pitching with each to feel the differences you achieve in height and length.

REDUCED BACKSPIN FROM ROUGH

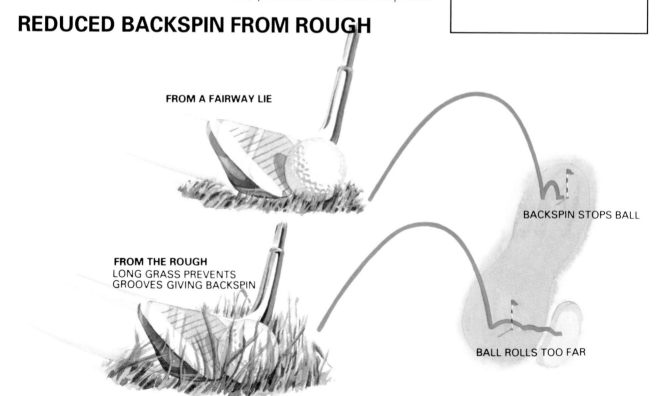

FROM A FAIRWAY LIE

FROM THE ROUGH
LONG GRASS PREVENTS
GROOVES GIVING BACKSPIN

BACKSPIN STOPS BALL

BALL ROLLS TOO FAR

You can't generate much backspin when playing from the rough. This is because blades of grass become trapped between the clubface and the ball and stop the clubface

grooves from imparting spin. This results in a 'flier' and the ball doesn't stop quickly on landing.

Keep this in mind when pitching from thick grass. Try to land your

ball a few yards further back than normal and let it run up to the flag. Remember to visualize your shot carefully when playing from the rough.

PLAYING A PITCH SHOT

1 ADDRESS POSITION
Open your stance by sliding your left foot back about 2in (5cm) but keep your shoulders, chest and hips parallel to the ball-to-target line.

2 TOP OF BACKSWING
Make about a three-quarter backswing. The exact length depends on the distance of the shot. Your weight moves from an even distribution at address to your right foot.

3 THROUGH IMPACT
Keep your left wrist firm and focus on striking the back of the ball. Don't scoop it. Just after impact the clubhead moves level with your hands for the first time.

4 COMPLETION OF SWING
Your weight transfers on to your left side which lets your upper body rotate to the left to face the target. The throughswing is the same length as the backswing.

pro tip

Maintain hand speed at impact

When pitching from a difficult or rough lie be sure to hit through the ball at an even tempo. Don't shy away from difficult shots. Be aggressive at impact – if your hands slow down you fail to strike through the ball correctly. This leads to a poor hit and you will be lucky if your ball reaches even halfway.

while your right remains passive. This is the single most important point in pitching because your left arm and hand pull the clubface through the ball and so control its speed and path.

Let your body rotate to the left on the throughswing and allow your left shoulder to rise. From an even distribution at address your weight moves on to your right foot on the backswing, and on to the outside of your left foot by the completion of the swing.

A FIRM IMPACT

Your hands must be firm at impact to give you clubface control, direction and feel. Many golfers flick at the ball in an effort to gain height. Not only is this bad technique, it is also unnecessary. It's the loft of the clubface that gives your ball height.

As you practise, note that the s and wedge imparts more backspin than either the pitching wedge or the 9 iron. It has the most loft and creates a steep swing plane with its short shaft.

However, when learning to pitch, concentrate on selecting the club that hits your ball the necessary distance with a three-quarter swing. If the pin is close to a hazard don't risk forcing a sand wedge up to a full swing just because it imparts more backspin and stops the ball quickly. Take a longer club and accept that your ball will roll further on landing.

At this stage concentrate on developing a repeatable swing with all three clubs. Your backswing and followthrough must be of equal length.

OUT OF THE ROUGH

Pitching from long grass (rough) provides its own special problems,

PLAYING FROM THE ROUGH

1 OPEN CLUBFACE AT ADDRESS
Open the clubface slightly at address and grip the club firmly. This limits the amount it slips in your hands as the clubhead cuts through the rough.

2 FOCUS ON BACK OF BALL
Take the club away smoothly and break your wrists immediately to steepen the angle of the swing plane. Focus on cleanly striking the back of the ball.

3 LEFT HAND FIRM IN ROUGH
Your left hand takes the strain at impact as the rough gets entangled with the clubface, which turns to the left. This is why you open the clubface at address. Keep your head down through impact.

4 WEIGHT MOVES ON TO LEFT SIDE
Your weight transfers on to your left foot on the followthrough and your body rotates to face the target. Try to maintain your tempo throughout the stroke.

although the basic technique remains the same.

As the clubface passes through the rough, the tall, thick grass acts as a barrier and tries to twist the club in your hand to the left (clubface closes). Your left hand feels a greater strain at impact than if playing a pitch from the fairway.

You must counter the extra pressure exerted on the clubhead – and your left hand – by gripping the

club a little more firmly and opening the clubface slightly at address. Be sure to keep an even tempo throughout the swing.

Grass gets entangled between the ball and the clubface. This is unavoidable, so concentrate on hitting down on the ball and making as clean a strike as possible. Your swing path, stance, and ball position do not change when playing from the rough.

Short and long pitch

Approach shots draw gasps of admiration – often tinged with a touch of envy – from the galleries at professional tournaments. Frequently finishing close and sometimes dropping in, the ball seems to have a magical attraction to the hole.

Take heart – any golfer can hit a good approach shot. You don't need bulging forearms, you don't have to possess awesome talent – you just need to have a grasp of

the fundamentals. You then have a technique that you can apply to a variety of situations from 100yd (90m) and in.

The short pitch from around 50yd (45m) – often played over some form of hazard – is a shot that frightens many golfers into making a mistake. You need maximum height and minimum roll – there's potentially quite a lot that can go wrong.

Unfortunately it's one of those

CONFIDENCE AND CONTROL
From 100yd (90m) and in, you should find the green every time, get the ball close sometimes and miss the target altogether very rarely. Success from this range hinges a great deal on confidence. However, equally important is control – you must never hit an approach shot flat out. Call on the services of your 9 iron or pitching wedge, grip down the club slightly and make a three-quarter swing.

DOWNHILL APPROACH

WHICH SHOT?
When the fairway slopes downhill to the green and there are no obstacles in the way, you're in the pleasing situation of having a choice of shots. Try to think of a hole on a course you know where the contours are similar, and imagine you're just under 100yd (90m) from the hole. Probably the best shot – and certainly the most consistent – is a low flying, three-quarter stroke with a 9 iron. This controlled shot helps you find the correct line, judge weight accurately, and lets the natural lie of the land sweep your ball down towards the hole.

1 NO FRILLS TECHNIQUE
Golf is such a precise game that you should take every opportunity to keep your technique simple. There are situations when you need to be creative, but there's no call for heroics on this shot. A straightforward address position offers you a technique that is least likely to go wrong – feet, hips and shoulders square to the target with the ball central in your stance.

KEY POINT:
Distribute your weight equally on both feet.

2 EASY BACKSWING
You don't want too many moving parts in your swing here – play a hands and arms shot. Concentrate on a one piece takeaway and keep the club low to the ground. Never pick the club up quickly – you create too steep an arc and are likely to make a poor shoulder turn.

KEY POINT:
Keep it smooth.

3 CUT DOWN BACKSWING
For a full shot this backswing would be far too short for comfort. In this instance it's the perfect position. Your knees should be comfortably flexed and your shoulders almost fully turned. A little more than half your weight is now on the right side.

KEY POINT:
The left wrist should be firm and in control of the club.

4 CONSISTENT TEMPO
The most important point to remember at the top of the backswing is that you maintain the same tempo on the way down. Whatever you do don't rush it – this is a major cause of miss-hit shots.

KEY POINT:
Feel the back of your left hand guiding the clubhead.

5 LEFT SIDE IN CHARGE
Make sure your left wrist is firm through the ball. This ensures that the clubface remains square both into and after impact. A front view provides a good example of how you should retain your height throughout the swing. The head is at exactly the same level now as at address – there's no lifting or dipping at any time.

KEY POINT:
Most of your weight should be on the left foot at impact.

6 BALANCE PRACTICE
The hard work has already been done, but don't be lazy on the followthrough. Concentrate on key points such as good balance and a comfortable followthrough position. This helps improve your overall tempo during the swing.

KEY POINT:
Your upper body faces the target on the followthrough.

ON THE WATERFRONT

1 FLY THE FLAG

With water guarding the front the trouble is all too apparent. The mental fear rather than any degree of difficulty is the downfall of some club golfers. However, from only 60yd (55m), a shot at the flag can make you a contender – if you have the technique you can play a very attacking and satisfying stroke.

KEY POINT:
Grip down the club to enhance control.

2 OPEN FOR COMFORT

A slightly open stance is a good idea when you play this shot – your sand wedge is the ideal club. Both combine to produce a higher, more floating trajectory than you would normally wish for. Take the club back along the line of your body and break your wrists earlier than normal – this creates a slightly steeper swing arc which is essential when you play any shot from rough.

KEY POINT:
Keep your right elbow tucked in close to your side.

3 SHOULDER TURN

Even on a relatively short shot you need to be certain of making a good shoulder turn – although not quite as full as you would with a driver in your hands. You may be tired of being told to turn your shoulders, but if you don't, you can guarantee the club is way outside the line and on too steep an arc – it's impossible to hit a good shot from there.

KEY POINT:
Point your left knee in towards the ball.

4 UP AND DOWN

A view down the line gives a good indication of how the club should remain on a consistent plane throughout the swing. Note that the hands are in a similar position halfway through the downswing compared to halfway through the backswing. The angle of the club must be different though – almost lagging behind in a position known as a late hit.

KEY POINT:
Keep your head behind the ball – don't lunge forward.

5 STRIKE DOWN

You need lots of height on this shot, so remember to strike down firmly into the bottom of the ball. Compared with the full swing the legs are quite passive. However, they still have a role to play – drive your knees forward through impact to help move your weight on to the left foot. This promotes a sharp downward blow.

KEY POINT:
Keep your hands ahead of the clubhead at all times.

6 DANGEROUS FLOATER

The action of the clubhead sliding through the grass under the ball gives this shot the high, floating trajectory you desperately need. Practise it often – this is a shot that can help you threaten the flag in a host of potentially dangerous situations, such as flying over a hazard.

KEY POINT:
Push the back of your left hand through to the target for as long as possible on the followthrough.

shots that can ruin your score if you play it badly, so you must have the ability to get it right – at least to the extent that your worst pitch finishes very close to the putting surface.

Your sand wedge is the ideal weapon from most lies. Don't make drastic alterations to your technique. Simply open your stance slightly and position the ball further back than normal to ensure a downward blow and crisp contact.

The one exception to this rule is when your ball rests on hardpan. You need a club with a sharper leading edge – such as an 8 or 9 iron – to nip it cleanly off the surface. A sand wedge tends to bounce off hard ground.

PIN POINT ACCURACY

As you move a little further away from the pin, it doesn't necessarily become harder to pitch your ball close.

Professionals probably hit as many shots near to the flag from 100yd (90m) as they do from half that distance. There's no reason why you shouldn't either – although don't expect such a high level of accuracy.

The first point to remember is that it doesn't matter what club you use, as long as the end result is good. This means placing the emphasis on control. There's nothing impressive about bashing a sand wedge to 20ft (6m), if you can knock the ball closer with a comfortable 9 iron.

There are several factors that dictate the type of shot you should play. In calm conditions on a plain, featureless hole you have a wide choice of strokes open to you. In general though, never feel you're using anything more than a three-quarter swing.

FAVOURED FLIGHT

It's easy to misjudge a pitch into a green that slopes uphill from front to back. Coming up short is usually the problem for most golfers. Keep backspin out of the shot – it doesn't favour you from this position.

The best policy is to take a less lofted club than usual so that the ball naturally has a bit of run on landing. Pitch it short, but still on the putting surface, and let the ball do the rest. This is your best chance of finishing close to the hole.

Try to avoid playing a high, floating shot in this situation. It demands a very precise stroke to finish close. If you pitch your ball only fractionally short, it's likely to come to an abrupt halt.

If the upslope is severe you may even spin the ball back towards you – particularly if the greens are soft and receptive. This is a disappointing result from a not particularly poor shot.

However, a high trajectory shot is ideal if the green slopes away from you. If you have a good lie you should be able to land the ball softly on the front of the putting surface and allow the slope to carry it gently down towards the hole.

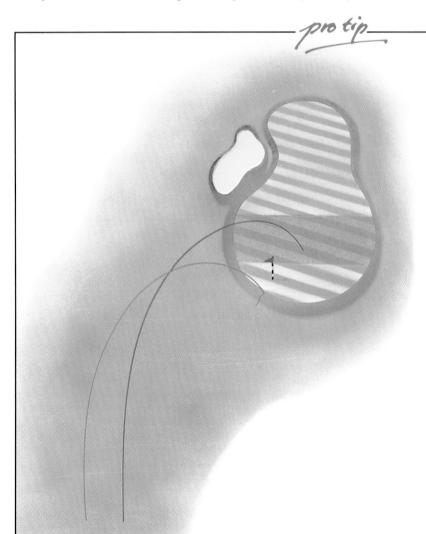

pro tip

Percentage pitch
When you're playing well and feeling confident, anywhere under 100yd (90m) can seem like an open invitation to attack the pin. But there are times when it's best to play the percentage pitch.

Raised greens look simple enough and certainly don't inject the same amount of fear as a deep bunker. However, they're cleverly designed, making approach shots deceptively hard. You need to be careful if there are any raised greens on your course.

With the flag positioned close to the front of the green, it's a potentially dangerous situation. Visualize a shaded area just beyond the pin – this is where you should pitch your ball.

Fire too strongly and you finish at the back of the green – play the shot a little too tentatively and you should still find the putting surface. Either way you have a putt rather than a chip for your next shot.

The worst fault is leaving your ball short because you then have to negotiate the slope a second time with your next shot. This is the heavy price you pay for being too impetuous.

Punch pitch

GREEN CONTROL
The punch pitch – one of the pros' favourites – is easy to control as your action produces a lot of backspin and the ball pulls up quickly on the green. Learning and being confident with this shot greatly increases your chances of getting up and down in 2 with your wedge – especially in a wind.

Controlling a wedge from the awkward distance of 50-90yd (45-80m) is a great asset. The punched pitch is the perfect shot to manoeuvre the ball through a wind from this range, but is by no means it's only use. All top golfers regularly hit this type of pitch both in windy and calm conditions to gain control.

The technique is simple and easily repeatable, which helps you play the stroke consistently well, provided you practise it. When hit properly the ball flies lower than a

PRECISE PUNCHING

1 BACK ADDRESS
Grip down the club slightly for more control. Align parallel to the target line. Position the ball back in your stance – just inside the right foot for a very low punch. Aim the blade square to the target, and push your hands ahead of the ball. Distribute your weight evenly.

2 FIRM WRIST TAKEAWAY
Take the club away smoothly with little wrist break. Though the shot is mainly a hands and arms stroke you must still turn you hips and shoulders during the backswing.

normal wedge and stops quickly on the green, as the way you strike the shot naturally creates much back-spin.

FAVOURABLE FLIGHT

The boring, penetrative flight is invaluable when firing into a head or crosswind, but is equally useful with the wind at your back.

Instead of hitting a pitch and run or a high floating shot – both trusting a little to luck – you can afford to attack the flag by playing the punch pitch. Even though you're hitting downwind the ball should pull up quite sharply, but allow for some run depending on the firmness of the green.

The spin comes from a sharp downward blow on a ball that's placed slightly further back in the stance than normal. The action of striking the ball before the turf is important for the shot to succeed. A touch fat and the ball runs on land-ing – as little spin is produced – and control is lost.

The ball stays low because it is placed back in the stance with your

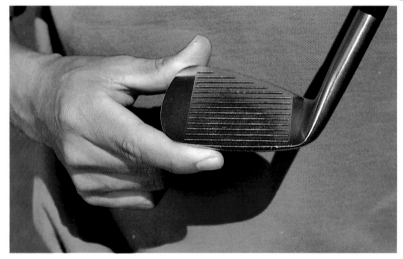

Wedge comfort
However good your technique is, you must also feel positive for the punched pitch to come off. For your confidence to be high it's vital to be comfortable with your wedge. There is no way that you can play the punch pitch well if your wedge doesn't suit you.

Knowing you have a club in your hand that you consistently strike out the middle of the face puts you in a positive frame of mind.

You may already have a favourite wedge -- often bought years ago – but if you don't, there are plenty of specialist wedges on the market. Finding a suitable one-off wedge means you needn't part with it when you change your set of irons.

3 SHORT AT THE TOP
Still keeping the wrists firm stop your backswing well short of parallel. Though the position at the top is not as long as usual, try to turn fully. Poor shoulder turn leads to an out-to-in downswing and a wayward shot.

4 SMOOTHLY DOWN
Swing down smoothly and keep your wrists firm. Too steep and wristy an attack makes the ball fly too high. Make sure your hands stay ahead of the clubface all the way to impact.

5 CRISP STRIKE
Lead the strike with your left hand and be sure to hit the ball before the turf. Keep your hands ahead of the clubface through impact and resist releasing, so the blade stays square for as long as possible.

6 SHORT AND BALANCED
Because you resist releasing your hands your extension is full and the followthrough short, which helps to keep the ball low and firing at the target. Don't stop too sharply as it leads to a stabbed shot. The finish should be balanced, with your weight fully on the left side.

hands forward, which delofts the clubface. The less wristy action than normal also helps to produce penetrative flight.

The punch pitch shot helps eliminate a miss-hit when playing under pressure, as the chances of hitting a thin or fat are less than with a straightforward pitch.

Reduced wrist action and having the ball placed further back in the stance both encourage crisp striking, so long as you don't dip too sharply on the downswing.

But for the shot to be accurate you must also be controlled on the followthrough. Lead with the left hand through the shot and avoid releasing too early. Try to keep the blade square to the target for as long as possible – this lessens the risk of a pull. Your finish position is much shorter than normal, but your whole action should be smooth.

WORK THE WIND

If you feel confident with this shot you can also shape the ball slightly to counter a crosswind. To produce a slight draw that holds on a left to right wind, stand a touch closed with the blade still square. But be sure not to use too much right hand as you could easily hit a hook.

If you open up your stance a fraction and keep the blade square the ball naturally fades slightly, which is useful in a right to left wind. The ball climbs a touch higher than the straight punch pitch and lands very softly – improving your control.

pro tip

Practice pitch
If you haven't tried to play the punch pitch before, it's sometimes hard to resist breaking your wrists on the backswing and through impact. One drill that is quick and easy to perform helps you naturally to keep the ball low and drilling.

Stick an umbrella into the practice ground, and pace out about 60yd (55m). From there, try to pitch balls – without bouncing – on to the umbrella and knock it over. This breeds an attacking and positive approach and helps you to hit the ball crisp and low – vital for punch pitch success.

José-Maria's wedge mastery

The brilliant Spaniard José-Maria Olazabal has worked his way to the top of world golf very quickly. His superb all-round game is capped by complete mastery of the wedge. He has tremendous natural flair and combines it with outstanding technique.

The punch pitch is an important weapon in Olazabal's armoury and makes him a deadly short game player. The dry, running fairways of Gleneagles in mid summer are the perfect surfaces for Chema to show off his prowess with the wedge. The short, controlled finish is a tell-tale sign of a low, spinning punched pitch shot that bites on the slick greens.

3

TRICKY SITUATIONS

Unfortunately, golf is far from straightforward, and a few tricky situations that you are sure to encounter sooner or later are featured here. Shots around the green have varying degrees of difficulty. You need to acquire feel and imagination; qualities that only come with practice. Technique and club selection are important considerations if you are to be successful at chipping.

David Frost finds a difficult lie during the 1988 US Open at Brookline, Massachusetts. Despite failure here, he won the Southern Open and the Tucson Open that year.

High cut-up shot

UP AND OVER
With a rough covered bank between you and the green, a high cut-up pitch is the only shot that gives you a realistic hope of getting up and down in 2. It removes as many elements of chance as you possibly can in golf. Use your sand wedge, stand open to the ball-to-target line and make a smooth, full swing. The clubhead slides through the grass and the ball flies high over the bank. If you judge the shot well, you can expect a soft landing on the green.

Take your pick
The key to good scoring is possessing a sharp touch around the greens. It's important to give yourself the best possible chance to excel in this department of your game, because it's the best way to knock strokes off your handicap.

Try carrying four short game clubs in your bag – a 9 iron, a pitching wedge and two sand wedges, one with standard loft and a second utility wedge with a few degrees extra. This range of clubs gives you great versatility around the greens.

Far too many club players' golf bags are heavily biased in favour of the long game. They might carry 3 different woods, plus a 1 and a 2 iron, but this is almost certainly too many long clubs. Analysed closely, most golfers would probably find they rarely use some of them.

There are a number of shots in golf that you play because there's no other way of finishing close to the hole. The high, cut-up pitch is a good example because it's often the only way to negotiate a hazard, hump, or other form of obstacle – situations where you cannot play a low flying shot.

With a high flight and soft landing, the cut up pitch is extremely satisfying when you play it well. However, many club golfers fail to succeed with this shot because they think drastic changes in technique are required to produce spectacular results.

This is simply not true. You need to make adjustments to your overall set-up and swing, but they should be only minor and based on the fundamentals of your normal full swing.

TEMPO IS THE KEY

A smooth swing is essential when you intend lobbing the ball high into the air. The cut-up shot is all about finesse and touch – you must feel in complete control of the clubhead at all times.

To vary the distance you hit the ball with the cut-up pitch, don't vary your tempo in the slightest. As you move closer to the flag, simply shorten your backswing and keep the same rhythm as you would for a longer shot.

Alternatively, grip further down the club – this means you don't have to make any other adjustments to your technique. Shortening the club narrows the arc of your swing which in turn reduces the distance you hit the ball.

If you feel you need to hit the ball hard to generate enough distance, you're probably too far out to play the cut-up pitch shot. It's impossible to maintain control of the ball if all you're thinking about is brute force.

KEEP IN CONTACT

Aim to achieve normal ball to turf contact. You shouldn't feel you need to hit down any more with this shot – your change in set-up and technique should naturally take care of this.

A mistake that many golfers commit is attempting to dig out a huge divot with the sand wedge – mainly because they try to hit down on the ball too hard. The result is a heavy duff. You may see Ian Woosnam knocking doormat divots down the Augusta fairways, but the turf is different to the type you probably play on, and Woosnam is an extremely powerful and talented golfer.

Backswing basics
The full sand wedge is a poorly played shot among many club golfers. Often hit flat out, with the emphasis on taking a divot like a doormat, this shot is miss-hit far more than it should be. The main problem is almost certainly trying to hit the ball out of sight – an effective cure for this fault lies in your backswing.

On the practice ground, find out how far you hit your sand wedge, but make only a three-quarter length backswing. Don't swing the club back all the way to horizontal at the top – that's when you start to lose control of the clubhead, and ultimately the ball.

Once you know the distance you hit your sand wedge, and the length of backswing required, you can play the shot with confidence when you're on the course. Never stray too far from this method – you can then develop a more consistent feel for distance from that crucial 100yd (90m) mark.

CUT ABOVE THE REST

1 SELECT YOUR SAND WEDGE
There's a steep rise in front of you, so you need to get the ball up quickly and land it softly on the green the other side. The cut-up chip is perfect, whereas other shots leave too much to chance. To play this master stroke, align slightly open and grip down your sand wedge for control. Make sure the clubface aims straight at the flag.

2 CLUB ON PLANE
Take the club back along a line parallel with your feet. When your hands are about waist high, the shaft of the club should point straight at the flag. Ask a friend to check this point for you – it's an indication that the club is on the correct plane at a crucial stage of the swing.

3 HOW FAR BACK?
Your top of backswing position should vary depending on the length of shot. From around the 50yd (46m) mark you should certainly take the club back beyond halfway – this ensures you can maintain a smooth tempo on the way down.

4 DOWNWARD ATTACK
Your first move from the top determines whether the shot is a success or a failure. You must pull the butt of the club down towards the ball – this sets the necessary angle between your left arm and the shaft of the club to ensure you strike down through impact and don't scoop at the ball.

5 SLIDE RULE
Imagine your left hand leading the clubhead through impact – you want to avoid releasing your hands so that the back of your left faces the target for as long as possible. From greenside rough you're not looking to strike the ball first – the clubhead slides through the grass, inflicting a cushioned blow at impact.

6 CHARGE HAND
Notice how the left hand pulls across the line from out to in through impact, not allowing the clubhead to pass the hands at any time. Make sure this is the way you finish every time you play the cut-up shot.

Deft chip from a bad lie

The rub of the green often seems to go against you. Think of when you have hit a half decent approach into a green but it just sneaks off and settles into a nasty little lie in the semi rough – often only a short distance from the flag.

Most handicap golfers curse their luck and become negative. Failing to get up and down is a natural result. Players who don't understand the technique needed to free the ball under control all too often fluff the shot or skull it way past the flag.

But there is no need for this dejection – it is possible to play a delicate chip that gives you an excellent chance of one putting.

Instead of hitting the ball before the ground – as with most chip shots – you need to hit firmly behind it. Play the stroke like a greenside sand shot. Whatever is directly behind the ball – perhaps a small clump of grass which prevents you from attacking it squarely – should be taken at impact.

STRIKING BEHIND

You should aim to hit about 1in (2.5cm) behind the ball – as you do in a bunker. This action ensures that the blade can slide under the ball and loft it out. This technique is especially useful on damp, heavy ground – where it is easy to hit a fat – as you can afford to be bold and take the muddy soil like sand.

Trying to strike the ball cleanly increases the risk of either fatting the ball or catching it thin.

For any delicate chip out of a poor lie to come off, you have to play the shot with conviction. Never be frightened – if your attack is firm and the followthrough is purposeful, you should have no problem in lofting the ball out, whatever is blocking it. Failure to swing fully usually leads to quitting on the shot and an uncontrolled stroke.

TROUBLE SPOT
Inconsistencies in the turf around a green can leave you an awkward lie when you least expect it. Sometimes the ball nestles annoyingly next to a clump of grass and prevents you from striking it cleanly. Opening your stance and playing the stroke like a commanding bunker shot pops the ball into the air and it lands surprisingly softly.

masterclass

Simpson's saving chip
The way in which a US Open course is set up is notoriously difficult. No player has ever been 10 under par at any stage of any event. This is mainly down to the punishing rough and the slick greens, which make controlling the ball hard. The short game is the hardest of all departments to master.

Hazeltine – the 1991 Open venue – stuck with this tradition, and tested the best to the full. In the play-off with Payne Stewart, Scott Simpson – winner in 1987 – had to pull off one of his best chips to keep his chances alive.

Coming to the tricky par 3 17th, the two were locked together. But Simpson cracked under the pressure and pulled his tee shot into a lake. He took a drop on ground trampled by spectators, and unluckily it settled into a poor lie. Scott then played a brilliant bunker style pitch to 8ft (2.5m) and sank the putt.

Taking the obstructing turf and the ball in one action meant he hit a delicate, soft landing chip. The shot limited the damage to only a bogey and kept him in contention with Stewart. Unfortunately another bogey at the last put paid to Simpson's attempt for another Open title.

SPLASHING FROM GRASS

1 SHARP PICK-UP
Position the ball as you would for a short greenside bunker shot – slightly forward of central. Align a fraction left of target but keep your blade square. Pick up the club quite sharply on the way back with just a hint of wrist break. This steep backswing naturally helps you attack the ball from an acute angle.

2 ACUTE AND FIRM
Swing along the line of your feet – so the path is slightly out to in – and attack downwards from a sharp angle. A shallow attack makes it hard to sweep through the grass behind the ball. Aim to hit about 1in (2.5cm) behind the ball. Keep your wrists solid, as a firm handed attack lessens the risk of a thin.

3 TAKE THE LOT
If you have struck down purposefully behind the ball with firm wrists, the clump of grass is taken along with the ball. And even though the grass was guarding the ball, the blade slides under it and pops it gently into the air.

4 SOFT RUNNING
Swing through firmly and fully, otherwise a fluffed shot can easily result. Even though the ball flies out quite high and lands softly, little backspin is produced with this shot – grass gets between the ball and clubface. So remember to allow for some run on the green.

Chipping up a two-tier green

S plit level greens have bam-boozled golfers all over the world ever since they were intro-duced early this century by the famed course architect Alister Mackenzie. Time after time ama-teurs fail to get up and down when chipping up a tier. It's usually down to a poor choice of shot.

The players that struggle most are those who just look at the distance and hit their usual style of chip. You mustn't ignore the slope however small the rise – even a gentle bank can affect the ball dramatically.

If you hit the wrong type of shot you might have to putt up and over the bank again with your next. If you overshoot you could be faced

with a tricky chip back – just a slight misjudgment and the ball could career away back down the slope.

Understanding the correct club and shot selections means you can tackle the chip with confidence and avoid big scores.

DOUBLE OPTIONS

For the best chance of holing your putt you must make sure your chip finishes on the top level. The per-centage shot is to play a straighter faced club – perhaps a 7 or 8 iron – and run the ball up the slope. The ball has more forward momentum than a high chip and so lessens the risk of the ball failing to reach the upper level.

STEP BY STEP
Practice and good visualization are the keys to understanding how to play up a two-tier green. You must know how certain shots behave if you want to overcome the slope. Try to imagine the path of the ball before you play a chip and run shot – it helps you gauge the pace. Always attack the shot confidently, as trying to be too cute can lead to disaster. Make sure that the ball reaches your target – 6ft (2m) past the hole is better than one that doesn't make the rise and rolls back towards you.

RUNNING CHIP

The low chip and run is easy to play and is the safest shot to combat a two-tier green. The risk of not reaching the upper level is lessened by a rolling ball which has momentum to climb the bank.

This type of shot is perfect for playing to a flag cut quite close to the step or downwind. Even if you have room to land a high wedge on the top tier, the ball may not stop because of the wind.

You can play the shot with anything from a 5 to a 9 iron. Your choice depends on the length of shot and how steep the bank is.

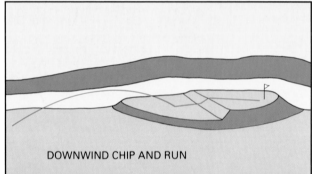

DOWNWIND CHIP AND RUN

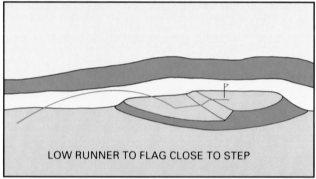

LOW RUNNER TO FLAG CLOSE TO STEP

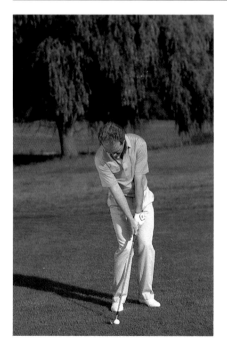

1 PLACED BACK
Grip down the club and push your hands forward. Position the ball back in your stance to ensure a good strike.

2 FIRM AND SHORT
Play the shot with a firm wristed action, and keep the backswing short. Lead the downswing with your left hand.

3 ABRUPT FINISH
Keep your hands ahead of the clubhead at impact, and stop short on the followthrough to help the ball stay low.

Low chip to kill

When there's a bank to clear between you and a hole near the front of the green, the perfect shot to play is the low chip to kill. You can play it from about 10yd (9m) to 40yd (36m) from the bank. You punch the ball into the bank, which kills the power of the shot. Then the momentum carries the ball up to the hole.

It's useful because chipping can be very difficult if there is little or no room to land the ball on the green *and* stop it near the hole. You have added problems if the ground is hard, when it's even more tricky to stop a fast-rolling ball in a small area.

FOCUSING YOUR SHOT

The key to playing this type of chip shot is visualizing just what will happen to your ball as it hits the bank. Look closely at the bank and how it is shaped. Its shape determines where you want the ball to make contact.

For instance, if your shot is straight, make sure you hit the correct part of the bank to keep your ball on line. Do not hit a part of the bank angled left or right – your ball will deflect off course, away from the pin.

Decide which club has the correct loft to hit your chosen spot on the bank. It's usually best to select a club with a small degree of loft. Most top players use the medium irons – 5, 6 or 7. Choosing a club with too much loft can be disastrous – you could fly the ball over the top of the bank and even overshoot the green.

Keep the picture of your shot clear in your mind at all times. Focus on the point of the bank you want to hit – cancel out all else.

THE TECHNIQUE

Align yourself slightly to the left (stance just open) with your feet close together. Set up with 60% of your weight on your left foot.

Your hands should be in front of the leading edge of your club throughout the stroke.

Play the shot with no wrist action, so that the ball does not fly too high and miss the bank. Gauge the length of your swing to suit your shot and make sure the back and throughswings are equal in length. This prevents the club slowing down just before impact.

Hit the ball firmly. Use enough force to keep it rolling after it hits the bank.

PUNCH IT POSITIVELY
Sometimes it's difficult to stop a normal chip by the pin (blue line). This may be because the hole is too near an obstacle, or because the ground is hard. If you have a bank in front of you, play a low chip to kill (red line). Take a club with the correct loft to hit the bank, and punch your shot firmly into it. The power of the shot is checked, but enough remains for the ball to run up to the hole.

A low chip into the bank lets you attack the pin.

A normal pitch is difficult to stop near the hole.

HITTING THE LOW CHIP

1 SET-UP
Set up with your weight slightly favouring your left foot. Grip further down the shaft than usual, with your hands ahead of the clubhead. Your feet should be close together, with the ball just right of centre in your stance.

2 BACKSWING
Make a half swing with your arms only – too much wrist action puts you in danger of sending the ball too high. Make sure your weight continues to favour your left side. Keep your head still and focus on your chosen spot on the bank.

3 IMPACT
Make sure your ball stays low by keeping your hands ahead of the clubface at impact. Try to create a feeling of your hands leading the clubhead into the shot. Keep your wrists firm and your head down through impact.

masterclass

Olazabal's deadly chipping

The brilliant young Spaniard José Maria Olazabal has fought his way into the European top flight by keeping cool under pressure. The greenkeeper's son learnt his golf by creating shots around the caddies' shed. It has left him with one of the most assured short games in the business and a magic touch with the low chip to kill.

Olazabal is now a master at attacking holes from around the green. The success of one of Europe's leading talents shows that practice with different clubs in different situations is the best way to improve your judgment of the low chip to kill. It also leads to the aggressive golf that wins matches.

4 THROUGHSWING
Your throughswing should be the same half swing as your backswing. Keep your clubface moving towards the target and your head down for slightly longer than after a normal stroke. A smooth rhythm from start to finish helps a clean strike.

Perched on the edge

Awkward stances are among the most unfair scenarios in golf, and there are few more upsetting than a precarious lie on the edge of – though not inside – a bunker.

You're faced with a testing recovery, having hit an acceptable previous shot. In these situations it's easy to dwell on your hard luck.

But it's essential you learn to accept your fate when things go against you, then tune your mind to the task at hand.

LIE AND DISTANCE

The lie is a crucial factor when you're considering which shot to play. If your ball is sitting well then

▼ WEIGHT ALLOWANCE
Maintaining your balance is the hardest part about this shot because the lip of the bunker pulls you towards the sand. Make allowances by keeping your head directly over the ball at address and throughout the swing - resist any swaying as this usually leads to a complete miss-hit.

CLOSE TO THE EDGE

1 BUILDING THE FOUNDATIONS
As soon as you find your ball in this position you should start thinking about how you intend taking your stance. One foot in the bunker is an option, but it lowers your right side a good deal. A far more secure stance is standing with your right foot as close to the bunker as possible. A little more than half your weight should naturally be supported by your right foot.

2 WEIGHT CENTRAL
Unlike any other full shot in golf, you must avoid transferring your weight away from the ball. If you do, you risk losing your balance altogether on the backswing. Apart from this one-off change in technique, your backswing should be the same as any other full shot.

count yourself lucky – this at least allows you a selection of clubs to choose from.

However, if the lie is bad any difficulties are worsened because you cannot stand normally to the ball. This restricts you in your choice of shots and you may have to accept that an ambitious recovery isn't on the cards.

Club selection also takes on a new perspective when you have an awkward stance. The distances you usually hit the ball have absolutely no bearing on the matter. You may hit a 6 iron from about 150yd (137m) on a flat lie, but if one foot is planted below the other you can probably afford to take two or three more clubs.

Your next concern should be how you intend keeping your balance. It's never easy, but there's usually a way of taking a fairly secure stance, and at the same time aiming in the general direction of the flag.

Experiment with a few different stances to find out which is most comfortable. Shuffle your feet around, try one foot in the bunker and one out, or perhaps vary the width of your stance if it helps.

Simulate the backswing you intend making to see if you can maintain your balance. It's best to restrict yourself to a three-quarter backswing. This is certain to improve your chances of remaining steady over the ball.

Very occasionally it's too risky to take a direct line at the flag. Your stance may be so awkward and your ball so precariously placed that you're in grave danger of hitting an air shot.

BAIL OUT

Only when these situations arise can you know when it's best to bail out sideways. Use your common sense and decide how much there is to gain by being adventurous. More importantly, how much do you stand to lose if the shot goes wrong?

There aren't many occasions when you have to resort to taking a drop. Even when your ball is so close to the edge that it seems to defy the laws of gravity, you can usually nudge it out sideways.

pro tip

Message from the master
Playing in a charity match with Sean Connery on the Old Course at St Andrews, Jack Nicklaus was once asked what he considered to be the most important factor to overcome in golf. 'It is an unfair game,' came the reply from the master.

If anything in golf is certain, it's that you are bound to have your share of bad luck. Perched on the edge of a bunker is one example – a cruel bounce is another.

Instead of cursing your misfortune, you'd do well to remember these wise words from Nicklaus. Because the golfer who brushes off bad luck is the one most likely to string together a good score.

3 PERFECT CONTROL
Restrict your backswing to three-quarter length to help you keep your balance. Notice how the left knee is more flexed than usual – this helps compensate for the fact that your right foot is below the level of your left. If you didn't make this adjustment you would almost certainly come up off the ball on the backswing.

4 STAYING DOWN
Your key thought at the start of the downswing is to prevent any sideways movement of your head – this is a little more difficult than normal because of the upslope which almost forces you backwards. Try to think of your head being positioned directly over the ball throughout the stroke.

5 NATURAL PROGRESSION
A good impact position and extension through the ball are the benefits of making the correct move from the top of the backswing. At this stage you should be able to draw a straight line from your eyes down to the point of impact.

6 EFFECTIVE STROKE
The followthrough may look ungainly, but at least you're not floundering in the sand. This is an indication that you've successfully kept your balance throughout the swing – in a very awkward position this is more than half the battle.

Back-handed chipping

Being stymied by a tree, fence or wall so you can't play an orthodox stroke to safety needn't mean taking a penalty drop.

Be inventive. Try turning a club around and playing the shot left handed, or face away from the target and hit the ball backwards. With ingenuity you can free yourself from trouble quite easily and accurately.

SECRETS OF SUCCESS

Playing the left handed shot successfully depends on your choice of grip and club, and the use of a steady and smooth action.

You can hold the club conventionally or adopt a left hander's grip. There is no hard and fast rule about which you should use – choose what makes you feel most comfortable and confident. As a guide, the longer the shot is, the easier it is to play with a left hander's grip – you can follow through more fully.

With short chips both grips are equally effective, as your swing is no more than a long putting action. Experiment on the practice ground to find the grip that gives you most control.

IN REVERSE
Most golfers class the left handed stroke with a turned round club as a trick shot reserved only for the professionals. Though this brazen stroke isn't part of your everyday shotmaking armoury, it's exactly the sort of shot that once in a while helps you escape from a tight spot. It looks impressive, too – and any player is capable of pulling it off given an understanding of the techniques and a confident approach.

LEFT HANDED CHIP

1 MIRROR IMAGE
Choose a lofted iron and turn the blade around. Your address is a mirror image of a right handed shot – align parallel to the target line, position the ball centrally and aim the clubface square.

2 CONTROLLED BACKSWING
With little other body movement, use your hands and arms to take the club away smoothly. Keep your wrist break to a minimum – especially on a short chip – to help co-ordinate the strike. The length of backswing depends on how far you need to hit the ball.

3 CRISP DOWNSWING
Swing down smoothly and firmly. Keep your body as still as possible to help the blade return correctly to the ball. The strike should be as normal – a crisp downward blow. Avoid a stabbing action.

4 FULLY THROUGH
Lead the throughswing with your right hand to keep the blade square for as long as you can. Follow through fully and don't quit. Failure to see the stroke through can lead to a fluffed shot.

Try out which club suits you best. Choose a lofted iron – anything from an 8 iron up. The lofted irons have shorter shafts, larger hitting areas and sit better on the ground than a longer iron. The way a wedge sits lets you play the ball from a central position and loft the ball easily.

SIMPLE SWING

Because co-ordination and striking are more difficult, the simpler the swing the better. You must keep steady throughout the stroke. The swing is mostly a hand and arms stroke – minimize other body movement to help execute the shot rhythmically.

The backwards escape is ideal for a long recovery shot because you can create more power than playing left handed. Simplicity is again the key. Swing with the right arm only, with little wrist break and no other body movement.

pro tip

Clubface choice
Club choice for chipping left handed is vital – usually, the more lofted the better. When you turn a wedge over, the area on which you can hit the ball is larger than on a straight faced club, giving more margin for error.

A wedge also has a shorter shaft, sits better on the ground than – for example – a 5 iron and you can position the ball centrally as normal. For a 5 iron to lie flat your hands have to be well ahead of the clubhead which makes co-ordinating a strike difficult. When you lay a turned over wedge square, its loft is perfect for chipping the ball out of trouble.

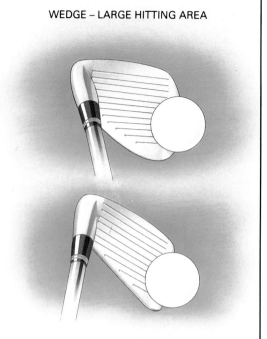

WEDGE – LARGE HITTING AREA

5 IRON – NARROW CLUBFACE

masterclass

Payne's predicament
To perform a successful left handed chip takes confidence and some skill. American Payne Stewart possesses a good deal of both.

On the tight, tree lined course at Shoal Creek – scene of the 1990 USPGA – defending champion Stewart had no hesitation in trying this specialist chip to save a shot. Fighting to stay with leaders Wayne Grady and Fred Couples, Payne had to try everything in his power to close the gap.

With a turned round wedge, Stewart managed to play a great recovery shot from a clump of trees at the 12th after a wayward drive. Payne's inventiveness kept him in touch, though he faded over the closing holes to finish eighth behind winner Grady.

BACKWARDS FACING STROKE

1 BACK TO THE TARGET
Choose a lofted club and grip down slightly. Stand square so that your back faces the target with the ball a few inches away opposite your right toe. Bend over from the waist just enough to see the ball easily. Aim the clubface square to target.

2 RIGHT ARM PICK UP
Pick the club straight up with little wrist break on a direct line away from the target. Keep the rest of your body still. How high you lift the club depends on how far you have to hit the ball.

3 DOWNWARD STRIKE
Swing down firmly but smoothly. Concentrate on striking the ball with a crisp downward blow and keep the blade square to target. It's important not to flick at the ball – let the natural loft of the clubface do the work.

4 LIMITED FOLLOWTHROUGH
You can't follow through too far or you strain your wrist and arm. But try to swing through as far as possible so you don't stab the ball or quit on the shot. Try to keep the blade square for as long as you can.

Chipping down to a two-tier green

One of the hardest shots to control in golf is the chip down a split-level green. Often the back section of a two-tier green is higher than the front section. If you overshoot the green with your approach shot when the flag is on the lower tier, it's tricky to get close to the hole with your next.

DELICATE TOUCH

To play this shot you need a different technique from that used for chipping up a two-tier green.

You take a straighter faced club for going up the green because you need run to get the ball on to the top tier. Use a delicate chip with a lofted club for the shot down the green. In this situation run is not important as the slope provides the pace on the ball.

The art of the shot is to put enough speed on the ball so that it almost comes to rest at the top of the downslope. From there the slope takes the ball down the bank and towards the hole.

What makes the shot harder is the fluffy grass usually found at the back of the green. It is easier to control a shot from the front of the green because you play off either fairway or a short fringe. It's harder to judge from the back as you can't get backspin and the ball runs on.

Play the stroke with a normal grip unless the ball is only just off the green when it's easier to use a putting grip. Use a short crisp swing. Throughout the stroke your weight should favour the left side. The key to success with this shot is practice.

FEEL, TOUCH AND CONFIDENCE
The shot requires a lot of thought, a sure touch and a little luck. Visualizing the shot well is half the battle, as where the ball lands and how far it runs are important. Be confident and play positively.

DEFT DOWNHILL CHIP

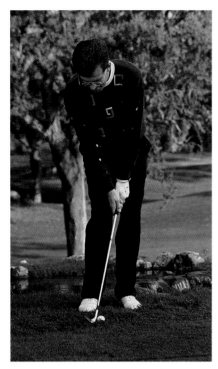

1 COMPACT STANCE
Adopt a narrow and slightly open stance. Grip your sand wedge about 1½in (4cm) from the top, and position the ball back in your stance. Your weight should be slightly on your left side.

2 LOFTED SHOT
Play the stroke firmly and don't quit on the ball. The natural loft of the sand wedge throws the ball up and it lands softly on the green. The thicker the grass you play from the more the ball runs.

3 JUDGING THE SLOPE
You should have judged the shot so that the ball rolls just to the edge of the slope. Play the ball higher with a more open clubface if the downslope is close – then you need as little run as possible.

masterclass

Laura Davies: power and finesse

Any top professional, whether male or female, must have a good short game, and Laura Davies is no exception. She is best known for her immense power, but she also possesses a great touch when she plays delicate chips on to the green.

Many women pros make up for their lack of length from the tees with deft chipping and putting. But Laura Davies has used both her tremendous power and great finesse to win many big events, including the 1987 US Women's Open.

4 LET THE SLOPE WORK
If you judged the shot properly the ball reaches the step at a slow pace and then runs downhill towards the hole. Take into account the steepness of the slope in judging how you play the shot.

LEARN FROM THE PROS

Practising your chipping will enable you to develop a reliable short game. You will encounter the same situations around the green many times over, so it is worth being prepared for the inevitable. We take a look at the approach of José Maria Olazabal and Ronan Rafferty. By studying their techniques carefully you can improve your short shots.

Playing from an island bunker during the 1990 Dunlop Phoenix Open, 'Tommy' Nakajima aligns his body well left of the target but aims his clubface square. The position helps him to gain extra loft – essential to ensure the ball lands softly on the green near the flag.

Chipping drills

At the end of the round it's the numbers at the bottom of your card that matter. If you want to score well your short game has to be in good shape. There are no prizes for hitting the ball brilliantly if your total doesn't match your striking ability on the day.

No golfer becomes a good chipper overnight, so take every opportunity to practise this part of your game – your short shots become sharper as a result.

As with all practice, it has to be constructive if you're to reap the full benefits from your efforts. There are probably more practice drills for chipping than any other aspect of golf, so it tends to be more enjoyable. The other advantage is you don't need a great deal of space to chip a few golf balls.

You may also have the boost of holing the occasional chip, which gives you lots of encouragement and spurs you on to hole even more. This form of practice has the psychological edge over hitting full shots – how often do you hole out from 150yd (135m)?

DEVELOPING DRILLS

The purpose of any chipping drill is to discover for yourself which shots work best for you. But there's always a lot to learn from the masters –·both in technique and how to visualize each shot.

Tom Watson is a great believer in playing chip shots with as little backspin as possible. He feels that it's easier to roll the ball smoothly and judge pace when there's very little spin on the ball. Only when it's absolutely necessary does Tom aim to stop the ball quickly – for example when there's not much green to work with.

WIDE REPERTOIRE
The best way to learn about shots from close range is to regularly spend time around the practice green. Experiment with different clubs and play a variety of strokes. If you have more than one shot up your sleeve your options are never limited. Whatever the situation, keep your hands ahead of the ball at address and accelerate the clubhead into impact.

MAKE THE CORRECT CHOICE

LEAVE THE FLAG IN...
Every golfer aims to hole greenside chips. While you can't achieve this every time, you can increase the number of shots that finish close by leaving the flag in. This encourages you to be more aggressive on the stroke – you know that even if you hit the ball a little too hard, there's always the possibility of it hitting the flag and occasionally dropping in. This is particularly helpful for downhill chips where the ball often gathers speed towards the hole. Even at pace the ball seldom rebounds too far away which means your putt is a short one.

...TAKE THE FLAG OUT
If you remove the flag when you chip, you have to judge weight very precisely. In the back of your mind you know the pace has to be spot on for the ball to stand any chance of going in. If you hit the chip too hard there's nothing to stop it – not even the back of the hole – and you're likely to be left with a long putt. You may also find that you leave a lot of chips short. Knowing the ball needs to be rolling gently if it's to drop prompts you to be tentative – which must be the furthest thought from your mind.

There's usually more than one way to play a shot from around the green – club selection is just as important as execution.

For every chip there are two targets you should consider – a precise landing area and the flag. The most accurate way to judge the weight of any chip is to first decide where you want to land the ball and then predict the roll. Don't make the mistake of concentrating *only* on the hole.

Select a hole on the practice green and play shots with a variety of clubs from the same spot. You quickly learn which club is best suited to the shot. You also find out which clubs make it hardest for you to chip the ball close.

An effective way to re-create an on course situation is to play shots to a variety of holes, all from the same spot. There are no second chances in a round of golf, so give yourself only one ball for each chip. This tests your ability to judge line and length at the first attempt. It's also a useful yardstick to assess the development of your touch and feel.

Another productive form of practice is to take a selection of clubs

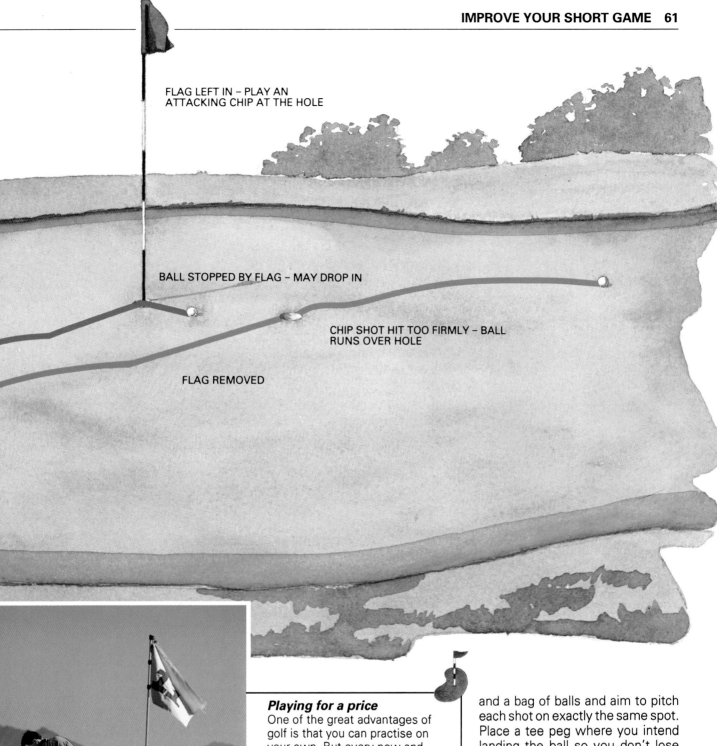

FLAG LEFT IN – PLAY AN
ATTACKING CHIP AT THE HOLE

BALL STOPPED BY FLAG – MAY DROP IN

CHIP SHOT HIT TOO FIRMLY – BALL
RUNS OVER HOLE

FLAG REMOVED

Playing for a price

One of the great advantages of golf is that you can practise on your own. But every now and then you need someone else around to help build a competitive edge into your game.

Chipping provides the perfect opportunity to bet with your friends. Playing for lunch or the first round of drinks is usually just the sort of incentive you need. The stakes aren't high, but no one likes losing.

Select nine different shots to play from around the practice green. The simplest game is playing closest to the hole – keep score as in a matchplay competition. Alternatively, treat each hole as a par 2 and play a mini strokeplay event with just your wedge and a putter.

and a bag of balls and aim to pitch each shot on exactly the same spot. Place a tee peg where you intend landing the ball so you don't lose sight of your objective.

Pay close attention to the differences between each shot – the height generated by each club, the amount of spin on the ball and how far it rolls on landing. This quickly develops your knowledge of chipping and makes it easier to visualize shots when you're on the course.

KEEP IT COMPETITIVE

Even if you're on your own, try to be as competitive as possible in your practice and always set yourself goals. If hitting balls is aimless, you're unlikely to see much of an improvement in your short game – you soon become bored with practising too.

Treat every chip as a potential matchwinner so that you put pressure on yourself to perform well every time.

Imagine you need to get up and down in two to win the most important competition at your home club. When it comes to the real thing you can look back on the hundreds of times you've been in that situation before – and played a good shot.

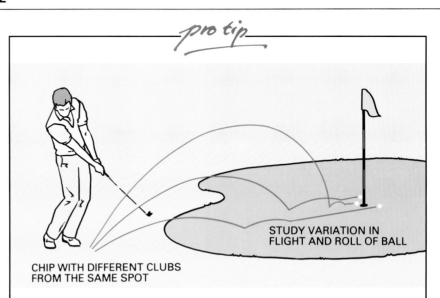

pro tip

CHIP WITH DIFFERENT CLUBS FROM THE SAME SPOT

STUDY VARIATION IN FLIGHT AND ROLL OF BALL

Choosing the right club

There's more than one way to play a chip shot. When you practise, take a dozen golf balls and play shots to the same hole with a variety of clubs. Only through a process of trial – and the occasional error – do you discover which shots give you the greatest success rate.

The higher the shot the less run there is on landing. This is ideal for floating the ball over trouble and is best played with a sand wedge. However, it's one of the more difficult strokes to play, so avoid the high chip unless you have no option.

Lower shots generate more run on the ball and are perfect when there's no trouble between you and the flag. Ideally, you want the ball running at the hole as smoothly as one of your finest putts. Any club from a 5 iron to an 8 iron gives you enough loft to clear the fringe with very little backspin, promoting roll.

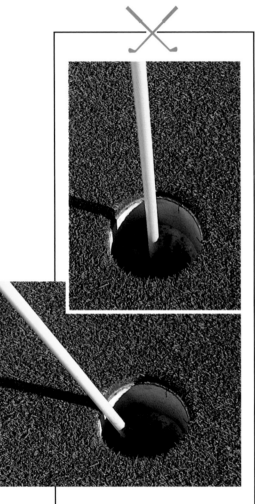

Straight up

When you're just off the edge of the green, check that the flag is standing perfectly vertical in its hole. This makes sure there's a big enough gap for the ball to drop in.

If the flag is leaning slightly towards you it can prevent your ball going in. The rules allow you to straighten the flag so that you're fully rewarded if you play a good shot. But don't be greedy – you're not allowed to deliberately lean the flag away from you.

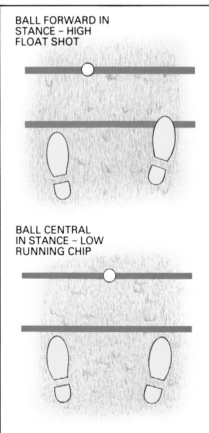

BALL FORWARD IN STANCE – HIGH FLOAT SHOT

BALL CENTRAL IN STANCE – LOW RUNNING CHIP

Altering ball position

Your stance and ball position have just as much bearing on a chip as the club you use. Subtle alterations to both enable you to vary your shots without changing your club.

If you want to float the ball high and stop it quickly, open your stance and position the ball just opposite your inside left heel. You can use your normal bunker shot technique to slide the clubhead under the ball, slightly out-to-in.

Playing the ball further back in your stance lets you use the same club to hit a lower shot. This is particularly helpful if the ball is sitting down in light rough.

Make sure the clubface is square to the target – this delofts the club and contributes to the lower trajectory of the shot. Break your wrists early on the backswing and strike down firmly with your hands leading into impact.

Sharpen your short game

The club golfer probably receives more snippets of advice on the short game than any other aspect of golf. Wise words inform the frustrated player that half the shots in a normal round are putts, and that you make your score around the greens.

This sort of advice alone is seldom enough to end the misery of the golfer who suffers from a poor short game. Knowing how to do it is one thing – putting it into practice is another.

Everything you do around the greens needs to be more precise and repeatable than on the other shots because there's less margin for error. For this reason alone it's essential to keep your technique as simple as possible.

OPTIONS OPEN

The quickest route to a complete short game is to develop a wide repertoire of shots around a variety of clubs. From close range always practise with a selection of clubs – you can then approach every situation with a choice of shots in your bag.

Some golfers practise around the greens with just one club, feeling this is the quickest route to proficiency and consistency. But if you restrict yourself to a favourite club for chipping you make the short game even more difficult for yourself.

For example, it's extremely hard to manipulate the flight and roll of a pitching wedge from a variety of lies and situations – you need impeccable feel and magical hands. The occasional master stroke is bound to come off, but there are likely to be more times when you struggle to hit the ball close.

TARGET PRACTICE
Knocking your short game into shape isn't simply a case of hitting pitches and chips on the practice ground – the often neglected greenside bunker shot is equally important. Grab a bag of golf balls and flip them on to the green from different lies. Try the hard shots as well as the easy and remember the basics – open stance with the clubface pointing at the flag.

HOW TO STAY IN CONTROL

1 FUNDAMENTAL RULES
Every time you approach a pitch shot think of
control – try saying the word to yourself if necessary,
as long as it's the uppermost thought in your mind.
Stand relaxed to the ball in a comfortable address
position – for a wedge shot the ball should be central in
your stance.

2 STROKE AND DISTANCE
The backswing serves more purpose than just
setting the club in the ideal position from which to
attack the ball. The length of backswing determines the
distance you want to hit a pitch shot. Halfway back
gives you lots of control and enough time to generate
clubhead speed.

Destructive force

Every golfer enjoys being in a situation where
attack is the best policy. After all, shooting for the
pin is a far more exciting prospect than playing
safely to the middle of the green.

From perfect position some golfers can be too
impetuous, swinging the club with such force and
aggression that they seem to be trying to bash the
cover off the ball. This tactic is ill-advised from any
range, but with a pitching wedge in your hands it's
perhaps the worst fault of all.

Co-ordination can easily desert you as the
followthrough becomes a frantic flail with your
arms. A solid strike can't be ruled out, but you
cannot possibly judge distance or accuracy on a
consistent basis if you're trying to hit the ball too
hard.

The most effective way to hit your ball close is to
swing within yourself – your short game is certain to
benefit. Factors such as brute force and aggression
are potentially disastrous in the golf swing.

3 IMPACT MIRRORS ADDRESS
The position of the left arm and club at impact is almost exactly the same as at address helping to ensure that the clubface returns to square. You can only achieve this consistently if your downswing is unhurried – clubhead speed is built up gradually rather than suddenly.

4 PUNCHED FOLLOWTHROUGH
You achieve this compact followthrough position by driving the back of your left hand towards the target. This helps keep the clubface square for as long as possible. Note how the followthrough is the same length as the backswing – a good habit to build into your game.

ESSENTIAL INGREDIENTS

The fundamentals are the same for most short shots:
● slightly open stance;
● hands positioned ahead of the ball at address;
● light but secure grip;
● length of swing that enables you to accelerate the clubhead smoothly into impact;
● clean contact with the ball.

Tempo and rhythm are just as important from close range as they are for the full swing – this is vital to a reliable short game. Tempo varies from one golfer to another. Study the top players and see how their tempo – although it differs from pro to pro – remains constant from tee to green.

Tom Watson has a brisk swing and keeps the same tempo all the way down to his putting stroke.

Fred Couples wields his driver with a slow, almost lethargic action – but like Watson, he too keeps the same rhythm for his short game.

You must also adopt a sound strategic approach to the short game – the mechanics without the mind is no guarantee of success.

SHORT SHOT STRATEGY

Every golfer should have a pre-shot routine, whether preparing to hit a drive or weighing up a chip from close to the green. Whatever system you choose, try to make it such an integral part of your game that it never varies.

A study carried out by the USPGA found the time it took some professional golfers to prepare for each shot – after the club was selected – varied by less than one second.

This is not so much a conscious effort on the part of the player – it's almost impossible to time yourself so precisely. This consistency results from good habits on the practice ground.

Part of your pre-shot routine for the short game should always be to visualize the stroke you want to play. Never hit a pitch or a chip without first targeting a precise landing area.

GAUGE THE BOUNCE

Make it easy to predict how the ball reacts on landing. Bear in mind that you're likely to get an even bounce if you pitch your ball on the green rather than off it. And whenever possible, land your ball on a flat area, not a slope.

With good mechanics and a sound approach you have the recipe for success. Both of these qualities lead to good feel – and it's feel that can make the crucial difference between a sharp short game and an untidy one.

Imaginary target

Firing approach shots into the pin is one of the spectacular benefits of having a sharp short game – not only do the shots look good, they do wonders for your score and your confidence.

While very few golfers are blessed with the ability to do this every time, everyone is capable of achieving this result a couple of times in a round. Whenever club golfers struggle with pitch shots, the problem is often something to do with length – the ball usually falls on the shy side rather than too long.

If you find this happens to you, it's not necessarily a flaw in technique – more a slight error in judgment. A bit of visualization can help you out.

Next time you're faced with a shortish approach into the green, picture an imaginary flag at the point where you intend landing your ball – probably just short of the flag in most cases. Try to pitch your ball on top of the imaginary flag. In your mind you are then playing an attacking stroke – albeit at a target that doesn't exist!

Using your imagination should enable you to get the ball up to the flag more often. It's also a great morale boost because it helps cut out the frustration of seeing endless approach shots fall short of the mark.

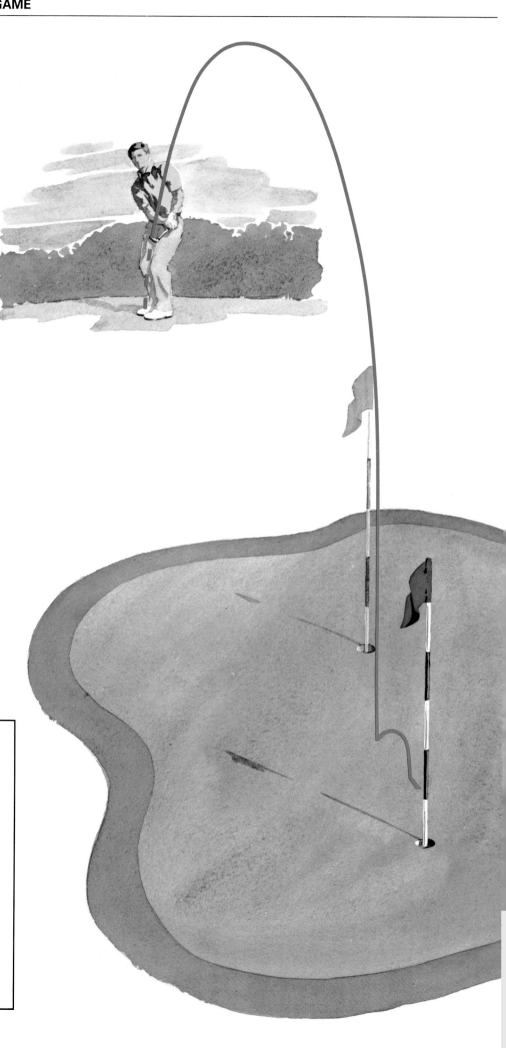

pro tip

Subtle adaptation

Before you choose which ball to use make a decision – do you play one that spins, or adapt your approach shots to allow for bounce and run? Sensible ball selection is often neglected by club golfers, at great expense to their scores. Make sure you play the right type of ball at all times.

A ball with a wound construction and soft cover is much easier to control than a two piece ball with a hard cover. Even Seve Ballesteros would struggle to stop a solid ball quickly on a firm green, so don't attempt to do so yourself.

masterclass

Olazabal's short game

Since bursting on to the world golfing scene in 1986 with two European Tour victories, José-Maria Olazabal has been renowned for his short game.

From the full wedge to a delicate chip around the green, he is one of the world's best. Place Ollie near the green and he stands a great chance of getting down in 2.

One of the reasons for his prowess is the way his golf devel-oped in his younger years. He was already playing off scratch in his early teens – he had to work on a razor sharp short game to compen-sate for his lack of length.

Practice is the key. Olazabal com-bined his natural ability with hours of practice to develop great touch and flair. He can stand in the same spot and play the ball in four or five different ways and still be dead on target.

WEDGE WONDERS
Olazabal plays the long and medium range pitch with precision and extreme control. He often hits the low punchy wedge. To practise this, position the ball back in your stance. Keep the clubface square and push your hands forward. A crisp strike sends the ball low. Be bold and pitch the ball just short of the flag – it checks quickly on the green.

CHIP AND RUN
José-Maria plays the running chip with an 8 or 7 iron and the simplest of techniques. He keeps his wrists firm and plays the shot with just his hands and arms. The object is to get the ball running quickly. It's much easier to judge the pace of the shot when the ball is rolling than it is chipping high to the flag.

DELICATE LOB
Every department of Olazabal's short game is excellent, but he is best known for his touch on delicate lobs. He grips lightly and lets his hands and arms control the shot. At address he aligns slightly left so he can open up the clubface for extra loft. For lower scores, spend half your practice time on developing short game feel.

From a distance of 80yd (73m) he is equally comfortable playing the normal three-quarter wedge, a low checking shot, a high lobbing sand wedge or the pitch and run. It's this versatility and vision that has made him the short game player he is.

FOLLOW OLLIE

Any golfer wanting to advance his or her game must refine pitching and chipping. A flexible short game can shave vital shots off your score.

You must spend time – like Olazabal – tuning your game from close range up to 110yd (100m) out. Be creative with your shot making. Experiment by hitting different shots from the same place with various clubs, and you should soon develop better touch and control.

Concentrate on visualizing the shot and playing it with an easy rhythm – whether it's a full wedge or a little chip and run. Use basic technique – this helps keep the stroke simple and improves your control.

pro tip

Perfect pitching
To improve your feel when pitching, it's a good idea to practise hitting balls from varying distances. It's fine to play from one spot and groove a swing, but this doesn't help you feel the shot.

Start from a point roughly 20yd (18m) from the green. Work your way back to about 80yd (73m) by dropping and playing a couple of balls from points about 20 paces apart. From each spot you must change the strength of your stroke.

This practice develops a sense of distance and touch. It's a vital asset when you're out on the course since you have only one chance to play a shot – you must sense instantly what stroke is needed.

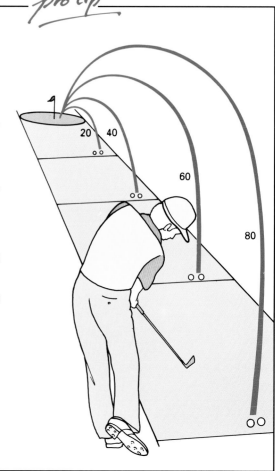

masterclass

Pitch with Rafferty

After a short but glittering amateur career, Ronan Rafferty has become one of Europe's leading professionals. A legacy from his unpaid days has held him in good stead ever since – an almost magical touch with the wedge.

To play at such a high level at so tender an age – Ronan was only 17 when he played in the Walker Cup – his short game had to be razor sharp to make up for his lack of length. Rafferty fine tuned his pitching, and from 50-90yd (45-80m) the Irishman is now one of the best on the Euro Tour.

Though Ronan has an individual style – quite a lot of hands and arms with a restricted leg action – you can learn lessons from his method.

His prowess stems from a superb rhythm. His swing is long, smooth and deliberate, but firm and controlled. Rafferty relies on his excellent timing and on the natural loft of the club to do the work – he never forces the shot.

CLEAN STRIKE

Unlike many of his fellow pros, Ronan's stock long range pitch takes little turf after striking the ball. He nips the ball off the fairway – a natural action, as the Irishman grew up on firm seaside fairways.

This clean, crisp striking method creates much backspin which heightens his control – even on the firmest of greens. But he does not hesitate to take turf if he needs to – perhaps for a punched pitch or out of light rough.

Rafferty stands fractionally open for every pitch. He feels that it helps him to keep the blade square to the target through impact, and he can resist releasing his hands too soon. This aspect of his method is one to copy – it improves your accuracy. Control the swing with your left hand, and guide the club with your right.

KEEP IT SMOOTH

Whatever type of pitch you play, try to keep balanced and steady. Excessive body movement and a snatchy action can only lead to a duffed shot. If you're too eager to watch the ball and come off the shot, it's easy to hit a thin. Trying to force a wedge can lead to a heavy shot.

Follow Ronan – stay still throughout the stroke and concentrate on a free flowing swing. Never attack the ball too aggressively – keep the rhythm the same for all lengths of shot. Simply vary the length of your backswing to judge the distance and use the same even tempo.

RONAN'S RISE TO THE TOP
Ronan Rafferty at last realized his full potential in 1989. Three tournament victories and several top ten finishes – including a 2nd place at the Dunhill British Masters at Woburn – helped him to grasp the No. 1 spot on the Order of Merit. He has an excellent all-round game with seemingly no weaknesses, but his strengths are definitely headed by his short game. Learn from Ronan's technique – you can add control and consistency to your short game by following his rhythmical action.